SIGN HERE:

Confessions of a Used Car Salesman

By

DANNY MEEKS

"Insider-tips that will save you thousands on your next car purchase!"

SIGN HERE: Confessions of A Used Car Salesman.

Copyright © 2015 by Danny W. Meeks.

All rights reserved, including the right to reproduce this book or portions thereof in any form.

ISBN-10:1505704995

First Edition
Published in USA.

Table Of Contents

ACKNOWLEDGEMENTS

1. ABOUT ME
2. HERE YOU ARE AT THE DEALERSHIP
3. TRADE-IN WOES
4. NEED VS. DESIRE
5. BEFORE WE GO ON
6. NEGOTIATING THE DEAL
7. FINANCE OFFICE (F&I)
8. SUB-PRIME LENDERS
9. ONE MORE SUGGESTION
10. BRINGING IT ALL TOGETHER

FINAL THOUGHTS

ACKNOWLEDGEMENTS

This book is dedicated to the countless sales people and sales managers who brought me to this point and gave me all the knowledge I am giving to you.... without realizing it might someday be used against them!

To my wife Lisa for editing my creative spelling and unconventional grammatical style!

Also to my brother, Stephen Meeks, who helped me realize what was holding me back. Together, we got me kick-started!

A huge "Thank you!" to my long-time friend Kathy White of *Moments by Kathy and David Photography* in

Gladewater, Texas for doing the cover photo! Great job!

ABOUT ME

My name is Danny Meeks, and I am a recovering car salesman. OK, let me explain that last part. I have spent the last 10 years as an officer of the county sheriff, but prior to that I was a salesman at a series of auto dealerships in the North Texas area. I was primarily a used car salesman from the mid to latter part of the 1990's through the end of 2004, and I was good at it. However, in the early part of 2004, I became tired of the whole game. In December of that year, I was offered a chance to go to work in law enforcement, and I took it.

During the years I spent in sales, I learned many things about the sales industry; in particular, of course, the auto sales industry. Being on the "inside" for so many years, I learned how to listen to what was being said to me and, above all, what to watch out for. Ten years later, I am constantly being asked by family and friends for advice when they are buying a new or used car, truck, or SUV. I decided to put this information into a portable form that they could access anytime they were in a position to need it.

I am offering this "**insider information**" to you here Do not mistake the length of this information for a lack of value. Every section has the ability to save you money….LOTS of money! The section on finance alone can save you thousands on your very next purchase! Certainly that is worth the few bucks you are spending to get ALL the information! I can assure you that some things never change and the old adage "knowledge is power" is absolutely one of those things! Here is that knowledge. Use your new power to your advantage!

    I sincerely hope you save a bundle on your next new or used vehicle purchase using the simple, yet powerful, insider tips you find here! Ready...Here we go!

D. Meeks (Uzedcarguy)

HERE YOU ARE AT THE DEALERSHIP

I'll bet you have seen this: You drive onto a dealership lot and there they are…the hoard of salespeople waiting to pounce on you! That makes some people uneasy and even scares them a bit. Having been on both sides of the aisle, I am now going to share a little something with you that you might not have stopped to consider: there's nothing to be scared of! They are simply perched up there waiting for a way to pay their electric bill or make their own car payment. Every person who drives up on the lot is a potential commission voucher and a step closer to making a living. Some may be more aggressive than others, but they are all there to earn a paycheck just like you are at your job. Remember…the more relaxed you are, the better your ability to stay alert and remember what you learned from these valuable insider tips! There is no law that says you can't have fun and enjoy your shopping experience. You are getting something for yourself. A GIFT! Why not have fun with it?!

      One more thing before we go any further: that automatic defense answer we all give when a salesperson asks if they can help us… "I'm just looking"… is fairly useless. Any salesperson worth his or her salt will remember his or her training and blow right past that objection. That's right. They are trained to ignore your "I'm just looking" statement. But that's okay because most of the time it's not true anyway! It's true that you are "looking" but you are looking with the end result of buying in mind. National averages show that 80+ % of people who go to the trouble of driving around looking at cars are going to buy within 72 hours. Sales professionals know that, and they are trained (and in many cases TOLD) to use that information to their advantage. That is also why some large, and even medium market dealerships threaten their sales people with being fired if they do not get basic follow-up information (name, address, phone number) and get you into the building so that a "manager" gets a chance to sell you on car if the salesperson can't. They may not sell you a vehicle, but it will not be from a lack of trying all possible options!

Just remember…The salesperson is not a monster. He or she is just an average guy or gal with a family and responsibilities and bills trying to make a living. It's the dealership that is forcing them to be pushy and aggressive to get the sale. I used to tell my potential buyers that "It's all part of *the game*." I promised not to hurt them, and in return they were not to act like I was an ogre or something! My favorite line of response to "I'm just looking." was "Great! That's exactly what I was doing when I found my wife!" Relax. You are going to be just fine, and you will end up with a great new vehicle!

TRADE-IN WOES

We should at least touch on this subject since most people have a trade when they decide to purchase another vehicle. If you do not have or anticipate having a trade just skip over this section. If you plan to trade in a vehicle on your next purchase you need to read it. It may save you money.

There are two ways dealerships make money on a trade. Obviously they can make money on the resale of your trade, provided your trade is not in such bad shape that they have to spend a lot to get it sale-ready. That is to say, the cost of repairs to your old car are not such that it can't be resold for a profit. The other way is what those in the industry call "holding on the trade". When dealers hold on the trade they are simply giving you less than the fair market value. Perhaps your trade is actually valued at $5000. The dealer tells you they will give you $4500. They have held $500. That is pure profit to the dealer.

You need to do your homework before heading to the lot. Know the fair market value of your vehicle! I do not mean what you think is the value of your trade. I mean know what it <u>actually</u> is. There are easy ways to find this value. In today's online world it is easier to do than ever! <u>www.NADA.com</u> or <u>www.KBB.com</u> (Kelly Blue Book) are just two of the web sites that can have valuable information about your trade value. There are probably many more. For the purpose of this writing, I will just list these two. These sites will allow you to input information about your current vehicle that will help determine final value. They will ask for mileage, equipment, year, etc. After entering this information, you will see several possible values ranging from poor condition to excellent condition. Each option will give guidelines for determining whether your vehicle fits into that category. Be sure you are brutally honest when determining where your vehicle fits! (DO NOT ask your banker what the value of your vehicle is. Unless he is going to write you a check, he could possibly mislead you unintentionally. Remember, your banker is trying to avoid hurting your feelings.)

Being prepared will simply keep your frustration level down when you see the numbers from the sales manager. No need to go into the situation with false hopes based on false information. Dealers may actually give you a little more than what these sites say for your trade if it is borderline between two different condition categories. It doesn't hurt to ask and it may just work! Just don't throw a fit if you don't get it. If you think you can make a little more by selling your trade yourself, you can always pull the trade and go with straight numbers on the new vehicle.

Another term the industry

throws around a lot is "over-allowing" on a trade. This is the practice of showing the customer a higher value for his or her trade than it is actually worth when working the numbers with the customer. For instance: A trade is worth an actual $5000. The customer is buying a vehicle that can be sold for $22,000. That is a trade difference of $17,000 plus TT&L (tax, title, and license). However, the customer has it in his/her mind and has divulged to his trained salesperson that the trade is worth $7500. The deal is written as a sale price of $24,500 for the new vehicle and $7500 for the trade. That is still a difference of $17,000 but the customer now feels better about the trade-in. This only works if the customer doesn't know the actual price of the purchase vehicle. ASK THE PRICE AHEAD OF TIME!

 I will pause here to address the elephant in the showroom. I would be doing you a disservice if I did not talk about the dreaded "UPSIDE-DOWN" situation we so often find ourselves in when trading in a vehicle. Upside down means you owe more on your trade than it is worth. What?! My car is only worth $5000 and I owe $10,000?! HOW!? Well... Did you roll your tax title and license into your loan? That can often add a substantial amount to your payoff (PLUS interest). Did you roll negative equity from your last trade in as well because you were upside down then too? See the way things can snowball?

  I used to advise my customers that a new vehicle drops about $5000 in value as soon as you "drive over the curb." That is because as soon as you sign the finance papers a new car becomes a used vehicle. There are ways to overcome the problem of being upside down. One is to make a decent down payment when making your purchase. Another way to break the cycle is to hold on to that trade, if possible, until it is paid off or at least in the last year of the loan repayment. That way there is positive equity in it. Third, never roll taxes and fees into your next loan! You can't drive taxes and fees, so why pay for them for five years along with your car or truck?

The most important things you can come away with from this section are: **DO YOUR HOMEWORK** and **BE HONEST WITH YOURSELF** when evaluating your vehicle. Does it need tires? That's $300 to $600, if not more, a dealer will have to spend on it to get it ready to sell. Does it have conditioning problems (Major dents, paint issues, etc.) ? Is it mechanically sound? Be honest. There is a reason most people want to get rid of their current vehicle. What is your reason? Also, understand that you may be upside-down and how to overcome it.

NEED V. DESIRE

While people buy a vehicle for a wide variety of reasons, they always have one that is driving them (pardon the pun) to the dealership. Are they tired of the old one? Is it too small? Too big? A gas guzzler? Not what they really wanted? Not what they really needed to do the job?

All too often, we buy on emotion rather than good sense. You know what I mean. We see a fire-red sports car, and our juices get to flowing. Our emotions start firing on all cylinders. We begin to imagine ourselves screaming down the road in that car, looking cool and feeling even cooler! We forget all about having two growing kiddos that have to have a little more leg room every few weeks. How much leg room did the salesman say was in that hot sports model again? You see where this is going? We buy on emotion, often forgetting logic and pragmatics. We buy a Corvette when what we need may be an SUV.

The same type of thing happens in buying a pick-up and larger trucks. We like the looks of that half-ton four-wheel drive, but what we need to actually pull our trailers is a ¾ ton diesel with two-wheel drive. Oh, but the salesman doesn't have one of those that we like. But there sits that half-ton 4WD with leather and all the amenities, and it's calling our name! So we go with the half-ton 4WD and hope for the best. Unfortunately, it strains to do the job once we get it home or to the job site. Soon there are transmission issues from overworking that undersized power-train (the parts that make it move like the motor, transmission, etc.). What we needed was to move up a class in truck. What we did was "settle." We allowed our emotions (and maybe even an overwhelming desire to get the car-buying trip over with quickly) to get the best of us. The best thing for us to do would have been to understand our

NEED vs. our DESIRE. We needed that ¾-ton, but we really liked that half ton.

ALWAYS understand your need when changing or just adding a vehicle. If it doesn't fit your need, all the "cool" in the universe will not make those monthly payments any easier to make. You may find yourself back in the market for a vehicle that does what you need. Only now you are likely "upside-down" in that cool car or undersized truck with the bad transmission you have to trade in!

BEFORE WE GO ON

Before we get into the section on negotiating, I think this is a good place to insert a little extra information that can save you money. It is well worth thinking about a vehicle with a minimal amount of miles and only one or two years on it as opposed to a brand new vehicle. If you want a new vehicle with no miles to speak of, then, by all means, look at new models. However, if you are okay with a vehicle that may be a year or two old and have, let's say, 15,000 miles on it, you can save a bundle!

These units used to be called "program" cars. Now they are simply lease returns, rental units that have been to auction, etc. No matter what they are called, they have taken that initial "hit" that comes from going from brand-new to used with the stroke of a pen. What I mean by that is someone else took the loss in equity when they bought the vehicle and then traded it in. The vehicle is now only a couple of years old and still in great condition. It has factory warranty left on it, and it is MUCH cheaper than a new one. These units are usually a great alternative for the budget minded buyer who wants to trade up to a later model.

As for buying brand-new vehicles…that is great, as well! Many times a company needs a write-off for tax purposes, and a new car or truck in the company name is a fantastic way to do that. Even if you are just the kind of guy or gal who only likes buying new, you are more than okay doing that if that is what you want to do! Look at rebates and incentives closely. You may be able to get that new unit for an incredible discount and save nearly as much as you would on one of those one- or two-year-old units! I am not trying to persuade you to go one way or the other. My purpose in this book is simply to show you ways to save money and keep from getting soaked in the process.

NEGOTIATING THE DEAL

Now we deal with the aspect of the purchase that most people dread: negotiating the deal. Many fear this more than anything. That is because they are either scared of it, or they feel awkward doing it. Neither should ever be the case. Remember, it is YOUR money you are trying to save! We will be dealing with several things that come up during the negotiation, so bear with me.

For the purpose of this book, I primarily assume we are looking at a pre-Owned (used) vehicle, but I will get to a HUGE tip on new vehicles in a moment, You will NOT want to miss it!

First things first, ask what the price is while on the lot. The best time for this is BEFORE the test drive. This keeps the salesperson from taking advantage of clues that you are more than a little interested in a particular vehicle. I must confess that I would occasionally quote a price that was higher than what my dealership was actually asking for the sole purpose of dropping that extra during the negotiation. That allowed the customer to feel that they were getting a far bigger discount and allowed me to make a bigger profit. (Hey…I told you I was a "recovering car salesman" when we started!) However, when asked about a price before I saw it as a vehicle my customer was interested in, I simply quoted the price it was listed for.

    It is worth noting that many dealerships "code" the price into the stock sticker on used vehicles. That is the sticker that lists the stock number and year of the vehicle and possibly other information. For instance, at one dealership I worked for, the bottom of the stock sticker would have something that read similar to this: 19FECD63. The first and last numbers (1 and 3) meant the price was $13,995. (We always added 995 to whatever the two numbers were.) A 2 and a 5 would mean $25 thousand and we add the 995. You get the idea. The second and next to last numbers were simply the year of the car. In the case of our example, it would be a 1996 model. You see how the sticker could be confusing to those who do not know what the sequence of numbers means. The letters had little, if any, meaning but were good camouflage. Again, a good sales person could tell you the "asking price" of the vehicle was $21,995 and give themselves some wiggle room during negotiations. You can see why knowing the price of the vehicle ahead of the test drive is a major plus for YOU during the process.

You can tip the odds in your favor even before you drive onto the lot. How? Simple. Every dealership with an inventory worth searching through has a web site these days. More of the "DO YOUR HOMEWORK" I spoke of earlier! Go to the dealer's website and shop before ever leaving the comfort of your home. Every dealer I ever worked for eventually had a web site, and, better still, they listed their best price on the site for each vehicle. They may have left a little room to negotiate but usually priced the vehicles thousands less than the asking price on the lot. That meant you did not have to depend on the salesman to give you the price. You knew when you left home!

If you shop via the internet, be sure to call the dealership before making the trip to see the vehicle. Many times the vehicle is sold over the phone or has a deposit placed on it by someone else who was smart enough to do their homework in this manner! Remember, the internet reaches many millions of people. On any given day, hundreds (at the minimum!) are seeing these cars and prices. Shopping online has another plus that makes it appealing to many buyers. The site will often have a section for potential customers to input their credit application information and thereby get pre-approval. That helps avoid the awkward situation when a person is turned down by lenders for a loan. We will touch on this more in the section on Finance and Warranties.

Now, back to the negotiation table.

The salesman will normally take some personal information, such as your name, address, and phone number. This is for future contact in the event you do not purchase a vehicle. There is a purpose for everything that goes on at the negotiation table. He will take the "work sheet" or "four square" to his manager. That is the guy who is working the numbers. No matter what has been quoted to you on the lot, the manager will be the only one writing numbers from where to start negotiating. The salesman will tell him what he quoted but the manager does the writing! (If you shopped via internet and saw a price you probably set up an appointment with the internet manager and would be dealing with him or her directly at this point.) Off the salesperson goes, to some mystical place where customers are not allowed. When they return, the work sheet is filled out and the game has begun! I know most folks hate "playing the game." I know because I heard that countless times. But folks, there is an old saying: "If ya don't wanna dicker, pay the sticker." Understanding ahead of time that there may be a short period of back and forth will lessen your stress. Relax and go with it. **You** will still win in the end! You don't have to buy if you don't like the numbers. It isn't that complicated. Dealerships have been operating in the same old way for a long time, and they aren't likely to change anytime soon. It's just part of the purchase process.

        The worksheet is most likely what has been called for decades a "four-square". That is because it is laid out in four sections. The top left square will show the "selling price". The top right square will show the amount allowed for your trade if you have one.

(By this time the salesman has already had your trade appraised by the manager or his assistant.) It will also show a "trade difference." The bottom left square will show a down payment suggestion. BEWARE! This "suggestion" is where dealers often make money that was *given up* in the selling price or trade value. The bottom right square will be where you need to pay close attention! That will show what your payments will be and for how long.

BE ADVISED! WARNING! NOTICE! PAY ATTENTION! OK... Now that I have your attention, I am about to give you one of the <u>biggest insider secrets</u> you will ever get or need. Most auto sales transactions are set up on five-year (60 month) loan terms. On a 60- month loan, every $25 of your payment is equal to approximately $1000 financed. In other words, a loan of $10,000 should be approximately $250 per month for 60 months.

Here's how this one simple tip

can save you THOUSANDS of dollars. Sales managers will never be specific about payments. They will give a "range," as they like to put it. For instance they will write your payments will as "450-475 @ 60." Let's not be naïve. That $450 is out the door the minute you agree to the range. You WILL be getting the $475 end of the deal! Now…let's back up a little. Let's say the figures are not something you like, so you say, "No way am I paying that!" The salesman marks through the 450-475. He may ask something like, "How close to this can you come?" You say, "I am not paying more than $350 a month." He/she writes down $350, then asks you, "up to…?" You will feel compelled to say "$360." At this point, a seasoned salesperson may say "But no more than…?" Do not fall into this trap. Remember, any number you give WILL be used against you in the end. The salesperson heads back off to "ask the manager." This give-and-take may go on for a while, but you get the picture.

Let's say the salesperson came back in this scenario and said, "We are close. I can't do the $360, but we can do $375-$385." At that point he makes an X on his work sheet and then places his pen by it and pushes it in your direction. Two things have just happened. First, they just did what is referred to as "a bump." That means they most likely can do what you asked and agree to your payment but they are trying one last trick to get a little more profit. Remember, that first number ($375) is out the window. It may as well not even be there. That $385 is what they want you to agree to. That is a $25 "bump". That is also an extra $1,000 you just paid for a vehicle you can actually get for less if you just say "No." The second thing they did was called "the silent close." When they put that pen down and pushed it toward you, they are supposed to shut up and remain silent. The old saying in the sales industry is "the first one who talks loses." If you agree, you lose. If the salesperson speaks, it can only result in a different price. Keep silent and wait them out! My suggestion would be to remain silent and simply mark out their price. Write down your $350-$360 and sign beside it. That tells them you are not paying the extra. If they can do the deal at your figure, they probably will. This is only true if you are within a small spread from them. Otherwise, you stick to your guns until they are closer to your figures. In the end, you will either get the payments you can live with or you walk away.

I should say at this point that you should use this tip to realistically know from the beginning what your payments are likely to be. In other words, if you are looking at a vehicle that is priced at $20,000, you are not going to get it for payments of $250….unless, of course you put down a pretty substantial down-payment!

You can also negotiate your trade value, but remember what I told you in the previous section on trade-ins. THAT is why it is important to know beforehand what your trade is actually worth. DO YOUR HOMEWORK.

Now…I promised a HUGE tip for buying new vehicles and here it comes!

Doing your homework when buying a new vehicle is simple and will only cost you about five bucks.

First step is to go to your local bookstore and purchase a copy of ***CONSUMER REPORTS: NEW CAR BUYER'S GUIDE*** . This magazine is a major information resource. It will list every vehicle made in the USA that year and will break down each one into dealer cost and retail price. You can see exactly what the dealer's cost is on a vehicle and what the sticker will show as MSRP (manufacturer's suggested retail price). The great thing about this publication is that it will allow you to look up dealer cost on the base model of the vehicle you want and then breaks down the options packages in the same way. One column lists the dealer cost and the other lists what it will show on the sticker price. You know going in what the dealer paid for the vehicle. That means you know what his mark-up is! This can't be done on used vehicles, but it is an awesome insider tip when buying new!

Guess what…the fun doesn't stop there! The next step in your homework is to go to the manufacturer's (Ford, Dodge, Chevy, etc.) web site. You can get information there like rebates currently available, dealer incentives and other discounts! Take those off the price you came up with through your magazine! Say a Ford vehicle is sticker priced at $23,700. You figured out that the dealer pays a cost of $19,585. Now, deduct the total of discounts, rebates , etc. available from the dealer cost. Let's say there were rebates and other monies that totaled $4,500. That means you are starting at a dealer cost of $15,085. You know he can't sell a vehicle without making at least a little profit, so you offer whatever you feel comfortable with as a profit. Let's say you offer him the $15,085 plus a profit of $500 plus taxes and fees. You saved a whopping $8115 just by spending a little at the bookstore. Well…that, and buying this book. That, by the way, will keep on giving every time you or a family member buys a vehicle, new or used!

THE FINANCE AND INSURANCE OFFICE (F&I)

Once you have made your vehicle selection and negotiated your price and payment, you will be taken to the F&I office. Finance and Insurance. Everyone has to go through this department whether they are paying cash, financing through the dealership, or any other means of purchase. This is where the contracts are drawn up and signed. It is also where many people lose money! Just because you were given an agreeable payment in the sales department doesn't mean you are through negotiating! Your salesman has likely put together a folder of your paperwork from the negotiating table, as well as a credit application and a credit history. He gives that to the F&I manager, who shops your credit around to multiple lenders in order to get the best rate for both you and the dealership. Your credit history has a score associated with it often referred to as a FICA score. This score is what lenders use to determine the APR (annual percentage rate) they will allow for your loan. The higher your score is, the lower your APR will be. The lower your APR is, the lower your payments will be!

This is where I urge you to pay close attention. The dealership is allowed by the lender to make money off of you in finance. This is referred to as "making money on the back end" of a deal. The price you negotiated on the car is the "front end". How does a dealership make money on the back end of a deal, you ask? Here's how. The lender gives the dealership a rate based on your credit score. This is referred to as a "BUY-RATE". That is the APR at which a lender is willing to loan you money. The finance guys can add up to three (3) percentage points to any buy rate other than those from sub-prime lenders. (More on that in a moment.) So let's say you have great credit. A lender agrees to a buy- rate of 4.9%. The finance manager will figure your actual payments on a rate of 7.9%! They will never tell you the actual buy-rate. They will only tell you the rate they are happy with. At this point, you should stop their spiel and tell them they are "going to have to do better than that." If they want your business, they will. Tell them you understand the game and how the "back end" works. What are they going to do? If they deny that they are doing it, they are lying to you, and you don't want to do business with them anyway, right? Offer them 1% over your buy rate. What is your buy rate again? Simply figure 3% less than what they tell you your payments are figured on. The banks/lenders will not allow them to go more than three percent over the buy rate and they WILL hit you for the full three percent over. Just drop 2% off the rate they quote you and everyone, especially YOU, gets a good deal.

Let's use some real numbers to get a real picture. Let's say you negotiate a deal where you are financing (including all monies financed-taxes, fees, whatever) $20,000 for a vehicle. The F&I manager says you were given a rate of 7.9% for 60 months. That makes your actual payments (using an amortization calculator) $404.57. Now... If he made the rate 5.9% your payments would be $385.73. Hey...20 bucks is 20 bucks! Over the life of the loan, you'd save $1200! Something else to consider is that if you just wanted to pay the extra $20 on the loan each month you would save even more by paying it off sooner!

Don't get too greedy. Remember, the dealership needs to make enough money from one source or another to keep the doors open and provide a service department in case you need repairs. One percent is not a lot.

Another way to get the best deal/rate in the finance office is to go in prepared! Talk with your bank before you even go looking for a vehicle. Get pre-approval if you are sure you will be buying soon. That way you get a rate from your bank and have that rate for leverage in the finance office. Let's say your bank agrees to loan you money on a new car at a rate of 4.9% or a used vehicle at 7.9%. When you get to the negotiation table, tell the salesman you have a rate of X from your bank. The sales manager will most certainly inform the F&I guys that they have to beat your rate if they want to get the finance business on your deal. Remember…they get paid on that part, too! Now, you are possibly looking at a rate of 3.9 or 6.9 depending on new or used vehicles!

Do not stop with just your personal bank. There are numerous lenders on-line that can give you a great rate as well. Most will email you the necessary paperwork to be taken to the dealership. Again, you have the leverage! Tell the guys at the dealership finance office the rate, if it is less than what they hit you with. If they want the business they will have to beat your best rate.

One last possibility is a credit union. Does your employer have or belong to a credit union? Often credit unions are small and therefore "hungry" for business. They will let you sign up for a small deposit in many cases. Once you are a member, you can check out their loan rates and other benefits.

SUB-PRIME LENDERS

Let's face facts for a moment. Most of us struggle financially at one point or another in our lives. Sometimes it affects our bill-paying, and that impacts our credit. We all know that the best credit gets the best rate on a loan, as I mentioned earlier. However, there is still hope for those who have less than perfect credit! This comes in the form of sub-prime lenders. These are lenders who will give a loan to people with a few blemishes on their credit history when the big banks will not. The thing to remember here is this: you are at their mercy. Everything I told you about negotiating a better rate earlier is out the window when dealing with a sub-prime lender. There is NO negotiating because they are more or less doing you a favor when no one else will touch your loan. Sorry folks, but it is what it is. The rates from sub-prime lenders are usually between 16 and 22 percent. I know! That

IS high. However you must remember these lenders are your last resort. The old saying in the auto sales industry is "you gotta buy back your credit". The good news there is that once you have used a sub-prime lender to purchase your vehicle you normally do not have as high an APR the next time, provided your payments are on time every month. THAT is a must!

Just throwing this out, but you should always go to your bank first even if you have had a few late payments or other reasonable blemishes. You never can tell how much weight your personal bank will put on your time with them. Many smaller banks will factor in how long you have done business with them, smaller loans you may have had with them, and whether or not you are willing to have a direct draft from your account. It is always worth a shot to ask them!

ONE MORE SUGGESTION: Extended Warranty and GAP Insurance

The last thing I will touch on is a topic most people go into a finance office dead-set against and then allow themselves to be talked into. I speak of the dreaded "extended warranty." This is honestly something you need to decide for yourself, but I am against them. I have purchased exactly ONE of these extended warranties in my life and it was a colossal waste of money. The one time I needed it, it was so much of a hassle that I decided to just get the car repaired somewhere else and forget the warranty! You do what you want. As for me and my house, we will not be laying out the huge tag-on money for an extended warranty ever again!

Now…That being said I will tell you of one F&I service/warranty I will never finance a vehicle (new or used) without. It is a smart move to purchase what is referred to as GAP INSURANCE. This is an insurance policy that does exactly what it sounds like. It fills a gap. When you finance your vehicle you immediately lose equity in it. We spoke of this in the earlier section. Now, let's say you have the misfortune of having a major accident in your new vehicle. The insurance adjuster says your vehicle is "totaled". The insurance company tells you the value of the wrecked vehicle is, let's say $6500. Unfortunately, you still owe $11,000! YOU are on the hook for that extra $4500 because they are only paying off the $6500! If you purchased GAP you can breathe easy. GAP insurance will cover the extra $4500! You can see the importance. I NEVER purchase a vehicle without GAP!

BRINGING IT ALL TOGETHER

Here is a simple scenario to give you an idea how it should all go in a smooth transaction.

As you approach the dealership you see a group of people perched along the front of the building. Do not be alarmed! They are harmless sales people trying to make a living. It is a dog-eat-dog world in the auto sales business so they are eager to help as many customers as possible.

Salesperson: Hi! Welcome to XYZ motors! My name is… And you are? (This is simply a way to get a person's name in the event they are reluctant to open up. It works, too!)

Customer: I'm John Doe. I'm just looking.

Salesperson: I understand. What are

you looking for?

Customer: I want a good used car.

Salesperson: Two or four door? Will there be more than two people riding in it at a time? (This series of questions will continue until a good idea of what the customer needs (or just wants) is established.)

Fast forward to the negotiation table.

Salesperson: Will you be trading something in today?

Customer: Yes. I have an old car out there that is paid for.

Salesperson: Great! I am sure we can get you a great value on it. Let's get started.

After the used car manager has looked at your trade, the actual negotiations begin.

Salesperson: OK, Mr. Doe, here's where we are. We will sell you our car for

$25,000. Fair market value on your trade is $4,000. That's a trade difference of $21,000 + taxes and fees. With just $3,000 down, your payments will be about $450-$500 for 60 months. Sign here by this X and we will get your paperwork started. (Places the pen by the X, pushes the paper toward customer and shuts up.)

Customer: (Scratches out the figures and says…) No. I am not putting more than $1000 down and I am not paying over $400 a month.

The salesperson leaves and takes the figures to his manager. He soon returns with new figures. If you stick to your guns, **WITHIN REASON,** you will end up with a new vehicle at a payment you can live with after a few of these managerial visits.

(If you are upside down in your trade you may have to be a little more open to a higher payment. As long as you understand that your payment will be higher than you expected because you have to roll the negative equity into your new loan you can sidestep some of the stress of the experience!)

Salesperson: OK, Mr. Doe. I have your paperwork ready to go to the F&I guys! Let's head that way.

(At the finance department)

F&I Mgr: Hi, Mr. Doe. I'm Jack, the Finance Manager. Let's take care of your contract and get you on the road in your new car! Are you ready?

Customer: Yes.

F&I Mgr.: I was able to get you a great low rate of 7.9% APR! Now let's talk about a few things before we have you sign any paperwork.

Customer: I have 7.5% at my bank and I am preapproved. What will that make my payments?

F&I Mgr.: If I can get you 7%, can I earn your business here with our finance office?

Customer: I am familiar with "back end" sales and I am thinking more like 5.9% myself.

At this point he either will or he will not. You do what your heart tells you to do. I personally would push for under 6.5% using this scenario.

F&I Mgr.: Mr. Doe, I have a few options I want to offer you on extended warranties. Let me go over them with you.

Again, it is your call at this point. I would think very carefully before making a decision.

Customer: I am not interested in those. I DO want GAP insurance. What will that do to my payments?

At this point it is just math. The numbers are not magic any more. Just breathe and relax. You are getting a new set of wheels!

FINAL THOUGHTS

There are many valuable resources for you to take advantage of, that were not available just a few short years ago. The internet is a HUGE vault of information! Here are just a few resources you may want to take a look at:

www.kbb.com (Kelly Blue Book for getting a value on a used vehicle or trade)

www.nada.com (National Auto Dealers Association also for values)

www.carfax.com (Fantastic source for information on a particular vehicle using the VIN number off of the vehicle. Tells you about major work done or recalls on them.)

www.eloan.com

www.chase.com/auto-loans

Many others!

I Hope you have learned something from what I have made available here. **I promise, you WILL save money using these insider tips!** Now...never again let the fear of the car-buying experience keep you from having fun and, above all, saving money while you do!

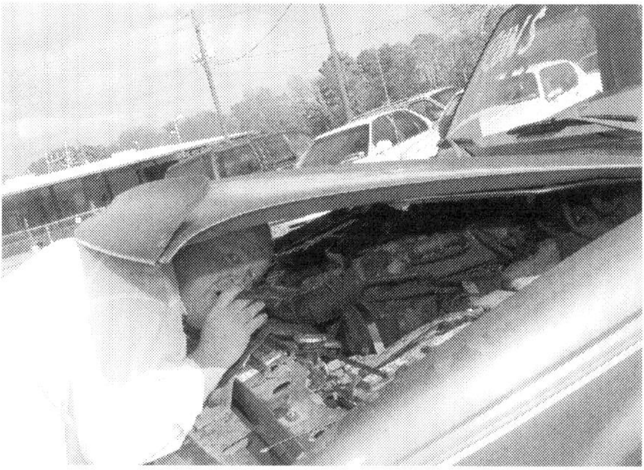

Made in the USA
Charleston, SC
16 January 2015